AN ENQUIRY INTO THE OBLIGATIONS OF
CHRISTIANS, TO USE

# MEANS FOR THE CONVERSION OF THE HEATHENS.

IN WHICH THE RELIGIOUS STATE OF THE
DIFFERENT NATIONS OF THE WORLD, THE
SUCCESS OF FORMER UNDERTAKINGS, AND
THE PRACTICABILITY OF FURTHER
UNDERTAKINGS, ARE CONSIDERED,

BY WILLIAM CAREY.

For there is no Difference between the Jew and the Greek; for the same Lord over all, is rich unto all that call upon him. For whosoever shall call on the name of the Lord shall be saved. How then shall they call on him, in whom they have not believed? and how shall they believe in him of whom they have not heard? and how shall they hear without a Preacher? and how shall they preach except they be sent?

PAUL

# INTRODUCTION

As our blessed Lord has required us to pray that his kingdom may come, and his will be done on earth as it is in heaven, it becomes us not only to express our desires of that event by words, but to use every lawful method to spread the knowledge of his name. In order to this, it is necessary that we should become, in some measure acquainted with the religious state of the world; and as this is an object we should be prompted to pursue, not only by the gospel of our Redeemer, but even by the feelings of humanity, so an inclination to conscientious activity therein would form one of the strongest proofs that we are the subjects of grace, and partakers of that spirit of universal benevolence and genuine philanthropy, which appear so eminent in the character of God himself.

Sin was introduced amongst the children of men by the fall of Adam, and has ever since been spreading its baneful influence. By changing its appearances to suit the circumstances of the times, it has grown up in ten thousand forms, and constantly counteracted the will and designs of God. One would have supposed that the remembrance of the deluge would have been transmitted from father to son, and have perpetually deterred mankind from transgressing the will of their Maker; but so blinded were they, in the time of Abraham, gross wickedness prevailed wherever colonies were planted, and the iniquity of the Amorites was great, though not yet full. After this, idolatry spread more and more, till the seven devoted nations were cut off with the most signal marks of divine displeasure. Still, however, the progress of evil was not stopped, but the Israelites themselves too often joined with the rest of mankind against the God of Israel. In one period the grossest ignorance and barbarism prevailed in the world; and afterwards, in a more enlightened age, the most daring infidelity, and contempt of God; so that the world which was once over-run with ignorance, now *by wisdom knew not God, but changed the glory of the incorruptible God* as much as in the most barbarous ages, *into an image made like to corruptible man, and to birds, and four-footed beasts, and creeping things.* Nay, as they increased in science and politeness, they ran into more abundant and extravagant idolatries.

Yet God repeatedly made known his intention to prevail finally over all the power of the Devil, and to destroy all his works, and set up his own kingdom and interest among men, and extend it as universally as Satan had extended his. It was for this purpose that the Messiah came and died, that God might be just, and the justifier of all that should believe in him. When he had laid down his life, and taken it up again, he sent forth his disciples to preach the good tidings to every creature, and to endeavour by all possible methods to bring over a lost world to God. They went forth according to their divine commission, and wonderful success attended their labours; the civilized greeks, and uncivilized barbarians, each yielded to the cross of Christ, and embraced it as the only way of salvation. Since the apostolic age many other attempts to spread the gospel have been made, which have been considerably successful, notwithstanding which a very considerable part of mankind are still involved in all the darkness of heathenism. Some attempts are still making, but they are inconsiderable in comparison of what might be done if the whole body of Christians entered heartily into the spirit of the divine command on this subject. Some think little about it, others are unacquainted with the state of the world, and others love their wealth better than the souls of their fellow-creatures.

In order that the subject may be taken into more serious consideration, I shall enquire, whether the commission given by our Lord to his disciples be not still binding on us,—take a short view of former undertakings,—give some account of the present state of the world, consider the practicability of doing something more than is done,—and the duty of Christians in general in this matter.

# AN ENQUIRY, &c.

## SECT. I.

*An Enquiry whether the Commission given by our Lord to his Disciples be not still binding on us.*

Our Lord Jesus Christ, a little before his departure, commissioned his apostles to *Go*, and *teach all nations*; or, as another evangelist expresses it, *Go into all the world, and preach the gospel to every creature*. This commission was as extensive as possible, and laid them under obligation to disperse themselves into every country of the habitable globe, and preach to all the inhabitants, without exception, or limitation. They accordingly went forth in obedience to the command, and the power of God evidently wrought with them. Many attempts of the same kind have been made since their day, and which have been attended with various success; but the work has not been taken up, or prosecuted of late years (except by a few individuals) with that zeal and perseverance with which the primitive Christians went about it. It seems as if many thought the commission was sufficiently put in execution by what the apostles and others have done; that we have enough to do to attend to the salvation of our own countrymen; and that, if God intends the salvation of the heathen, he will some way or other bring them to the gospel, or the gospel to them. It is thus that multitudes sit at ease, and give themselves no concern about the far greater part of their fellow-sinners, who to this day, are lost in ignorance and idolatry. There seems also to be an opinion existing in the minds of some, that because the apostles were extraordinary officers and have no proper successors, and because many things which were right for them to do would be utterly unwarrantable for us, therefore it may not be immediately binding on us to execute the commission, though it was so upon them. To the consideration of such persons I would offer the following observations.

First, If the command of Christ to teach all nations be restricted to the apostles, or those under the immediate inspiration of the Holy Ghost, then that of baptizing should be so too; and every denomination of Christians, except the Quakers, do wrong in baptizing with water at all.

Secondly, If the command of Christ to teach all nations be confined to the apostles, then all such ordinary ministers who have endeavoured to carry the gospel to the heathens, have acted without a warrant, and run before they were sent. Yea, and though God has promised the most glorious things to the heathen world by sending his gospel to them, yet whoever goes first, or indeed at all, with that message, unless he have a new and special commission from heaven, must go without any authority for so doing.

Thirdly, If the command of Christ to teach all nations extend only to the apostles, then, doubtless, the promise of the divine presence in this work must be so limited; but this is worded in such a manner as expressly precludes such an idea. *Lo, I am with you always, to the end of the world.*

That there are cases in which even a divine command may cease to be binding is admitted—As for instance, if it be *repealed*, as the ceremonial commandments of the jewish law; or if there be *no subjects* in the world for the commanded act to be exercised upon, as in the law of septennial release, which might be dispensed with when there should be no poor in the land to have their debts forgiven. Deut. xv. 4. or if, in any particular instance, we can produce a *counter-revelation*, of equal authority with the original command, as when Paul and Silas were forbidden of the Holy Ghost to preach the word in Bythinia. Acts xvi. 6. 7. or if, in any case, there be a *natural impossibility* of putting it in execution. It was not the duty of Paul to preach Christ to the inhabitants of Otaheite, because no such place was then discovered, nor had he any means of coming at them. But none of these things can be alledged by us in behalf of the neglect of the commission given by Christ. We cannot say that it is repealed, like the commands of the ceremonial law; nor can we plead that there are no objects for the command to be exercised upon. Alas! the far greater part of the world, as we shall see presently, are still covered with heathen darkness! Nor can we produce a counter-revelation, concerning any particular nation, like that to Paul and Silas, concerning Bythinia; and, if we could, it would not warrant our sitting still and neglecting all the other parts of the world; for Paul and Silas, when forbidden to preach to those heathens, went elsewhere, and preached to others. Neither can we alledge a natural impossibility in the case. It has been said that we ought not to force our way, but to wait for the openings, and leadings of Providence; but it might with equal propriety be answered in this case, neither ought we to neglect embracing those openings in providence which daily present themselves to us. What openings of providence do we wait for? We can neither expect to be transported into the heathen world without ordinary means, nor to be endowed with the gift of tongues, &c. when we arrive there. These would not be providential interpositions, but miraculous ones. Where a command exists nothing can be necessary to render it binding but a removal of those obstacles which render obedience impossible, and these are removed already. Natural impossibility can never be pleaded so long as facts exist to prove the contrary. Have not the popish missionaries surmounted all those difficulties which we have generally thought to be insuperable? Have not the missionaries of the *Unitas Fratrum*, or Moravian Brethren, encountered the scorching heat of Abyssinia, and the frozen climes of Greenland, and Labrador, their difficult languages, and savage manners? Or have not English traders, for the sake of gain, surmounted all those things which have generally been counted insurmountable obstacles in the way of preaching the gospel? Witness the trade to Persia, the East-Indies, China, and Greenland, yea even the accursed Slave-Trade on the coasts of Africa. Men can insinuate themselves into the favour of the most barbarous clans, and uncultivated tribes, for the sake of gain; and how different soever the circumstances of trading and preaching are, yet this will prove the possibility of ministers being introduced there; and if this is but thought a sufficient reason to make the experiment, my point is gained.

It has been said that some learned divines have proved from Scripture that the time is not yet come that the heathen should be converted; and that first the *witnesses must be slain*, and many other prophecies fulfilled. But admitting this to be the case (which I much doubt[1]) yet if any objection is made from this against preaching to them immediately, it must be founded on one of these things; either that the secret purpose of God is the rule of our duty, and then it must be as bad to pray for them, as to preach to them; or else that none shall be converted in the heathen world till the universal down-pouring of the Spirit in the last days. But this objection comes too late; for the success of the gospel has been very considerable in many places already.

It has been objected that there are multitudes in our own nation, and within our immediate spheres of action, who are as ignorant as the South-Sea savages, and that therefore we have work enough at home, without going into other countries. That there are thousands in our own land as far from God as possible, I readily grant, and that this ought to excite us to ten-fold diligence in our work, and in attempts to spread divine knowledge amongst them is a certain fact; but that it ought to supercede all attempts to spread the gospel in foreign parts seems to want proof. Our own countrymen have the means of grace, and may attend on the word preached if they chuse it. They have the means of knowing the truth, and faithful ministers are placed in almost every part of the land, whose spheres of action might be much extended if their congregations were but more hearty and active in the cause: but with them the case is widely different, who have no Bible, no

---

[1] See Edwards on Prayer, on this subject, lately re-printed by Mr. Sutcliffe.

written language, (which many of them have not,) no ministers, no good civil government, nor any of those advantages which we have. Pity therefore, humanity, and much more Christianity, call loudly for every possible exertion to introduce the gospel amongst them.

# SECT. II.

*Containing a short Review of former Undertakings for the Conversion of the Heathen.*

Before the coming of our Lord Jesus Christ the whole world were either heathens, or jews; and both, as to the body of them were enemies to the gospel. After the resurrection the disciples continued in Jerusalem till Pentecost. Being daily engaged in prayer and supplication, and having chosen Matthias, to supply the place of Judas in the apostolic office, on that solemn day, when they were all assembled together, a most remarkable effusion of the Holy Spirit took place, and a capacity of speaking in all foreign languages was bestowed upon them. This opportunity was embraced by Peter for preaching the gospel to a great congregation of jews and proselytes, who were from Parthia, Media, Elam, Mesopotamia, Judea, Cappadocia, the proconsular Asia, Phrygia, Pamphylia, Egypt, Lybia, Crete, Arabia, Rome, &c. and at the first effort God wrought so powerfully that three thousand were converted, who immediately after were baptized, and added to the church. Before this great addition they consisted of but about *an hundred and twenty persons*, but from that time they continually increased. It was but a little after this that Peter and John, going up to the temple, healed the lame man; this miracle drew a great multitude together, and Peter took occasion while they stood wondering at the event, to preach Jesus Christ to them. The consequence was that five thousand more believed.

This was not done without opposition; the priests and sadducees tried all the methods they could invent to prevent them from preaching the gospel. The apostles, however, asserted their divine warrant, and as soon as they were set at liberty addressed God, and prayed that a divine power might attend their labours, which petition was heard, and their future ministry was very successful. On account of their necessities who were engaged in this good work, those amongst them who had possessions, or goods, sold them, and devoted the money to pious uses.

About this time a man and his wife out of great pretensions to piety, sold an estate, and brought part of the money to the apostles, pretending it to be the whole; for which dissimulation both he and his wife, were struck dead by the hand of God. This awful catastrophe however was the occasion of many more men and women being added to the church. The miracles wrought by the apostles, and the success attending their ministry, stirred up greater envy in the priests and sadducees, who imprisoned them; from which confinement they were soon liberated by an angel; upon which they went immediately as they were commanded and preached in the temple: here they were seized, and brought before the council, where Gamaliel spake in their favour, and they were dismissed. After this they continued to prosecute their work, rejoicing that they were counted worthy to suffer shame for the name of Christ.

By this time the church at Jerusalem was so increased that the multiplicity of its temporal concerns was the occasion of some neglects, which produced a dissatisfaction. The apostles, therefore, recommended to the church to chuse seven pious men, whose office it should be to attend upon its temporal affairs; that *they might give themselves to prayer, and the ministry of the word.* Seven were accordingly chosen, over whom the apostles prayed, and ordained them to the office of Deacons by imposition of hands: and these things being settled the church increased more and more. One of these Deacons, whose name was Stephen, being a person of eminent knowledge and holiness, wrought many miracles, and disputed with great evidence and energy for the truth of Christianity, which raised him up a number of opponents. These soon procured his death, and carried their resentment so far as to stir up such a persecution that the church, which till now had been confined to Jerusalem, was dispersed, and all the preachers except the apostles were driven thence, and went every where preaching the word.

A young man whose name was *Saul,* was very active in this persecution; he had been educated under Gamaliel, a member of the Sanhedrim, was a person of promising genius, by profession a Pharisee, and much attached to the jewish ceremonies. When Stephen was stoned he appeared much pleased with it, and had the custody of the clothes of his executioners; and from that time was fired with such a spirit of persecution himself, that he went about dragging some to prison, and compelling others to blaspheme the name of the Lord Jesus. Neither was he contented with exercising his rage at Jerusalem, but went to the chief priests and obtained testimonials of authority to carry on the same work at Damascus. But on his way, as he was almost ready to enter into the city, the Lord changed his heart in a very wonderful manner; so that instead of entering the town to persecute, he began to preach the gospel as soon as be was able. This presently brought upon him the same persecution which he had designed to exercise upon others, and even endangered his life, so that the brethren found it necessary to let him down the city wall in a basket by night, and so he escaped the hands of his enemies. From thence he went to Jerusalem where he preached the word, but being persecuted there, he went to Cesarea, and from thence to Tarsus.

In the time of this trouble in the church, Philip went and preached at Samaria with great success, nay so great was the work that an impostor, who had deceived the people with legerdemain tricks for a long time was so amazed, and even convinced, as to profess himself a Christian, and was baptized; but was afterwards detected, and appeared to be an hypocrite. Besides him a great number believed in reality, and being baptized a church was formed there. Soon after this the Lord commanded Philip to go the way which led from Jerusalem to Gaza, which he did, and there found an eunuch of great authority in the court of Ethiopia, to whom he preached Christ, who believed, and was baptized; after which Philip preached at Ashdod, or Azotus.

About the same time Peter went to Lydda, or Diospolis, and cured Eneas of a palsy, which was a mean of the conversion not only of the inhabitants of that town, but also of the neighbouring country, called Saron, the capital of which was Lasharon; and while he was there, a circumstance turned up which tended much to the spread of the truth. A woman of Joppa, a sea-port town in the neighbourhood, dying, they sent to Lydda for Peter, who went over, and when he had prayed she was raised to life again; which was an occasion of the conversion of many in that town. Peter continued there preaching for some time, and lodged at the house of a tanner.

Now another circumstance also tended to the further propogation of Christianity, for a Roman military officer who had some acquaintance with the Old Testament Scriptures, but was not circumcised, was one day engaged in prayer in his house at Cesarea, when an angel appeared to him, and bid him send for Peter from Joppa to preach in his house. Before this the work of God had been wholly confined to the jews, and jewish proselytes, and even the apostles appeared to have had very contracted ideas of the Christian dispensation; but now God by a vision discovered to Peter that Christianity was to be spread into all nations. He accordingly went and preached at the house of Cornelius, at Cesarea, when several were converted, and baptized, and the foundation of a church laid in that city.

Some of the dispersed ministers having fled to Antioch in Syria, began to preach to the greeks in that city about the same time, and had good success; upon which the apostles sent Paul and Barnabas, who instructed and strengthened them, and a church was formed in that city also, which in a little time sent out several eminent preachers.

In the Acts of the apostles we have an account of *four* of the principal journies which Paul, and his companions undertook. The first, in which he was accompanied by Barnabas, is recorded in the xiii. and xiv. chapters, and was the first *attack* on the heathen world. It was a journey into the lesser Asia. In their way they passed over the island of Cyprus. No sooner had they entered on their undertaking, than they met with great difficulty; for Mark, whom they had taken as their minister, deserted them, and returned to Jerusalem, where, it seems, he thought he should enjoy the greatest quiet. Paul and Barnabas however went forward; in every city they preached the word of the Lord, entering into the jewish synagogues and first preaching Christ to them, and then to the gentiles. They were heard with great candour and eagerness by some, and rejected by others with obstinacy and wrath, and cruel persecution. One while they had enough to do to restrain the people from worshipping them as gods, and soon after, Paul was stoned, dragged out of the city, and left for dead. Having penetrated as far as Derbe, they thought proper to return by the way that they came, calling at every city where they had sown the good seed, and finding in most, if not all these places, some who had embraced the gospel, they exhorted and strengthened them in the faith, formed them into a church state, and ordained them elders, fasted and prayed with them; and so having commended them to the Lord on whom they had believed, returned to Antioch in Syria, from whence they first set out, and rehearsed to the church all that God had done with them, and how he had opened the door of faith to the gentiles.

About this time a dispute arising in the churches concerning circumcision, Paul and Barnabas were deputed to go up to Jerusalem, to consult the apostles and elders on the subject. This business being adjusted, they, accompanied with Judas and Silas, returned to Antioch with the general resolution, and continued there for a season, teaching and preaching the word of the Lord.

Paul now proposed to Barnabas, his fellow-labourer, that they might visit their brethren in the places where they had been already, and see how they did. To this Barnabas readily acceded, but a difference arising between them about taking *John Mark* with them, who had deserted them before, these two eminent servants of God were parted asunder, and never appear to have travelled together any more. They continued however each to serve in the cause of Christ, though they could not walk together. Barnabas took John, and sailed to Cyprus, his native island, and Paul took Silas, and went through Syria and Cilicia to Derbe and Lystra, cities where he and Barnabas had preached in their first excursion.

Here they found Timothy, a promising young man, whom they encouraged to engage in the ministry.

Paul being now at Lystra, which was the boundary of his first excursion, and having visited the churches already planted, and delivered to them the decrees of the apostles and elders relating to circumcision, seems to have felt his heart enlarged, and assayed to carry on the glorious work of preaching the gospel to the heathen to a greater extent. With Silas and Timotheus he in his second journey[2] took a western direction, passing through Phrygia, and the region of Galatia. Having preached the word in these parts with considerable success,[3] he and his companions wished to have gone into the proconsular Asia, and afterwards assayed to go into Bythinia; but begin forbidden of the Holy Ghost, who seems to have had a special design of employing them elsewhere; passing by Mysia they came down to Troas on the sea-coast. Here a vision appeared to Paul, in which he was invited to go over to Macedonia. Obedient to the heavenly vision, and greatly encouraged by it, they with all speed crossed the Egean Sea, and passing through the island of Samothracia, landed at Neapolis, and went from thence to Philippi, the chief city of that part of Macedonia. It was here that Paul preached on a Sabbath day to a few women by a river side, and Lydia, a woman of Thyatira, was converted and baptized, and her household with her. It was here that a poor girl, who brought her employers considerable profit by foretelling events, followed the apostles, had her spirit of divination ejected, on which account her masters were much irritated, and raised a tumult, the effect of which was, that Paul and Silas were imprisoned. But even this was over-ruled for the success of the gospel, in that the keeper of the prison, and all his house, were thereby brought to believe in the Lord Jesus Christ, and were baptized.

---

[2] The account of this second journey into the heathen world begins at Acts xv. 40. and ends chap. xviii. 22.

[3] See ch. xviii. 23. and Gal i. 2.

From Philippi they passed thorough Amphipolis, Apollonia, Thessalonica, (now Salonichi,) Berea, Athens, and Corinth, preaching the gospel wherever they went. From hence Paul took ship and sailed to Syria, only giving a short call at Ephesus, determining to be at Jerusalem at the feast of the passover; and having saluted the church, he came to Cesarea, and from thence to Antioch.

Here ended Paul's second journey, which was very extensive, and took up some years of his time. He and his companions met with their difficulties in it, but had likewise their encouragements. They were persecuted at Philippi, as already noticed, and generally found the Jews to be their most inveterate enemies. These would raise tumults, inflame the minds of the gentiles against them, and follow them from place to place, doing them all the mischief in their power. This was the case especially at Thessalonica, Berea, and Corinth. But amidst all their persecutions God was with them, and strengthened them in various ways. At Berea they were candidly received, and their doctrine fairly tried by the Holy Scriptures; and *therefore*, it is said, *many of them believed.* At other places, though they affected to despise the apostle, yet some clave unto him. At *Corinth* opposition rose to a great height; but the Lord appeared to his servant in a vision, saying, *Be not afraid, but speak, and hold not thy peace, for I am with thee, and no man shall set on thee to hurt thee; for I have much people in this city.* And the promise was abundantly made good in the spirit discovered by Gallio, the proconsul, who turned a deaf ear to the accusations of the jews, and nobly declined interfering in matters beside his province. Upon the whole a number of churches were planted during this journey, which for ages after shone as lights in the world.

When Paul had visited Antioch, and spent some time there, he prepared for a third journey into heathen countries, the account of which begins Acts xviii. 23. and ends chap. xxi. 17. At his first setting out he went over the whole country of Galatia and Phrygia in order, strengthening all the disciples; and passing through the upper coasts came to Ephesus. There for the space of three months, he boldly preached in the jewish synagogue, disputing, and persuading the things concerning the kingdom of God. But when the hardened jews had openly rejected the gospel, and spake evil of that way before the multitude, Paul openly separated the disciples from them, and assembled in the school of one Tyrannus. This, it is said, continued for the space of two years, *so that all they who dwelt in* the proconsular *Asia heard the word of the Lord Jesus, both jews and greeks.* Certain magicians, about this time were exposed, and others converted, who burnt their books, and confessed their deeds. So mightily grew the word of the Lord, and prevailed.

After this an uproar being raised by Demetrius, the silversmith, Paul went into Macedonia, visited the churches planted in his former journey, and from thence passed into Greece. Having preached up and down for three months, he thought of sailing from thence directly to Syria; but in order to avoid the jews, who laid wait for him near the sea coast, he took another course through Macedonia, and from thence to Troas, by the way of Philippi. There is no mention made in his former journey of his having preached at Troas; yet it seems he did, and a church was gathered, with whom the apostle at this time united in *breaking of bread.* It was here that he preached all night, and raised Eutychus, who being overcome with sleep, had fallen down, and was taken up dead. From hence they set sail for Syria, and in their way called at Miletus, where Paul sent for the elders of the church of Ephesus, and delivered that most solemn and affectionate farewell, recorded in the 20th chapter of the Acts of the Apostles. From hence they sailed for Tyre, where they tarried seven days, and from thence proceeded to Jerusalem.

Paul's fourth and last journey (or rather voyage) was to Rome, where he went in the character of a prisoner. For being at Jerusalem he was quickly apprehended by the jews; but being rescued by Lysias, the chief captain, he was sent to Cesarea to take his trial. Here he made his defence before Felix and Drusilla, in such sort that the judge, instead of the prisoner, was made to tremble. Here also he made his defence before Festus, Agrippa, and Bernice, with such force of evidence that Agrippa was almost persuaded to be a Christian. But the malice of the jews being insatiable, and Paul finding himself in danger of being delivered into their hands, was constrained to appeal unto Caesar. This was the occasion of his being sent to Rome, where he arrived after a long and dangerous voyage, and being shipwrecked on the island of Melita, where he wrought miracles, and Publius, the governor, was converted.

When he arrived at Rome he addressed his countrymen the jews, some of whom believed; but when others rejected the gospel, he turned from them to the gentiles, and for two whole years dwelt in his own hired house preaching the kingdom of God, and teaching those things which concern the Lord Jesus Christ, with all confidence, no man forbidding him.

Thus far the history of the Acts of the Apostles informs us of the success of the word in the primitive times; and history informs us of its being preached about this time, in many other places. Peter speaks of a church at Babylon; Paul proposed a journey to Spain, and it is generally believed he went there, and likewise came to France and Britain. Andrew preached to the Scythians, north of the Black Sea. John is said to have preached in India, and we know that he was at the Isle of Patmos, in the Archipelago. Philip is reported to have preached in upper Asia, Scythia, and Phrygia; Bartholomew in India, on this side the Ganges, Phrygia, and Armenia; Matthew in Arabia, or Asiatic Ethiopia, and Parthia; Thomas in India, as far as the coast of Coromandel, and some say in the island of Ceylon; Simon, the Canaanite, in Egypt, Cyrene, Mauritania, Lybia, and other parts of Africa, and from thence to have come to Britain; and Jude is said to have been principally engaged in the lesser Asia, and Greece. Their labours were evidently very extensive, and very successful; so that Pliny, the younger, who lived soon after the death of the apostles, in a letter to the emperor, Trajan, observed that Christianity had spread, not only through towns and cities, but also through whole countries. Indeed before this, in the time of Nero, it was so prevalent that it was thought necessary to oppose it by an Imperial Edict, and accordingly the proconsuls, and other governors, were commissioned to destroy it.

Justin Martyr, who lived about the middle of the second century, in his dialogue with Trypho, observed that there was no part of mankind, whether greeks or barbarians, or any others, by what name soever they were called, whether the Sarmatians, or the Nomades, who had no houses, or the Scenites of Arabia Petrea, who lived in tents among their cattle, where supplications and thanksgivings are not offered up to the Father, and maker of all things, through the name of Jesus Christ. Irenaeus, who lived about the year 170, speaks of churches that were founded in Germany, Spain, France, the eastern countries, Egypt, Lybia, and the middle of the world. Tertullian, who lived and wrote at Carthage in Africa, about twenty years afterwards, enumerating the countries where Christianity had penetrated, makes mention of the Parthians, Medes, Elamites, Mesopotamians, Armenians, Phrygians, Cappadocians, the inhabitants of Pontus, Asia, Pamphylia, Egypt, and the regions of Africa beyond Cyrene, the Romans, and Jews, formerly of Jerusalem, many of the Getuli, many borders of the Mauri, or Moors, in Mauritania; now Barbary, Morocco, &c. all the borders of Spain, many nations of the Gauls, and the places in Britain which were inaccessible to the Romans; the Dacians, Sarmatians, Germans, Scythians, and the inhabitants of many hidden nations and provinces, and of many islands unknown to him, and which he could not enumerate. The labours of the ministers of the gospel, in this early period, were so remarkably blessed of God, that the last mentioned writer observed, in a letter to Scapula, that if he began a persecution the city of Carthage itself must be decimated thereby. Yea, and so abundant were they in the three first centuries, that ten years constant and almost universal persecution under Dioclesian, could neither root out the Christians, nor prejudice their cause.

After this they had great encouragement under several emperors, particularly Constantine and Theodosius, and a very great work of God was carried on; but the ease and affluence which in these times attended the church, served to introduce a flood of corruption, which by degrees brought on the whole system of popery, by means of which all appeared to be lost again; and Satan set up his kingdom of darkness, deceit, and human authority over conscience, through all the Christian world.

In the time of Constantine, one Frumentius was sent to preach to the Indians, and met with great success. A young woman who was a Christian, being taken captive by the Iberians, or Georgians, near the Caspian Sea, informed them of the truths of Christianity, and was so much regarded that they sent to Constantine for ministers to come and preach the word to them. About the same time some barbarous nations having made irruptions into Thrace, carried away several Christians captive, who preached the gospel; by which means the inhabitants upon the Rhine, and the Danube, the Celtae, and some other parts of Gaul, were brought to embrace Christianity. About this time also James of Nisbia, went into Persia to strengthen the Christians, and preach to the heathens; and his success was so great that Adiabene was almost entirely Christian. About the year 372, one Moses, a Monk, went to preach to the Saracens, who then lived in Arabia, where he had great success; and at this time the Goths, and other northern nations, had the kingdom of Christ further extended amongst them, but which was very soon corrupted with Arianism.

Soon after this the kingdom of Christ was further extended among the Scythian Nomades, beyond the Danube, and about the year 430, a people called the Burgundians, received the gospel. Four years after, that Palladius was sent to preach in Scotland, and the next year Patrick was sent from Scotland to preach to the Irish who before his time were totally uncivilized, and, some say, cannibals; he however, was useful, and laid the foundations of several churches in Ireland. Presently after this, truth spread further among the Saracens, and in 522, Zathus, king of the Colchians encouraged it, and many of that nation were converted to Christianity. About this time also the work was extended in Ireland, by Finian, and in Scotland by Constantine and Columba; the latter of whom preached also to the Picts, and Brudaeus, their king, with several others, were converted. About 541, Adad, the king of Ethiopia, was converted by the preaching of Mansionarius; the Heruli beyond the Danube, were now made obedient to the faith, and the Abasgi, near the Caucasian Mountains.

But now popery, especially the compulsive part of it, was risen to such an height, that the usual method of propagating the gospel, or rather what was so called, was to conquer pagan nations by force of arms, and then oblige them to submit to Christianity, after which bishopricks were erected, and persons then sent to instruct the people. I shall just mention some of those who are said to have laboured thus.

In 596, Austin, the monk, Melitus, Justus, Paulinus, and Russinian, laboured in England, and in their way were very successful. Paulinus, who appears to have been one of the best of them, had great success in Northumberland; Birinnius preached to the West Saxons, and Felix to the East Angles. In 589, Amandus Gallus laboured in Ghent, Chelenus in Artois, and Gallus and Columbanus in Suabia. In 648, Egidius Gallus in Flanders, and the two Evaldi, in Westphalia. In 684, Willifred, in the Isle of Wight. In 688, Chilianus, in upper Franconia. In 698, Boniface, or Winifred, among the Thuringians, near Erford, in Saxony, and Willibroad in West-Friesland. Charlemagne conquered Hungary in the year 800, and obliged the inhabitants to profess Christianity, when Modestus likewise preached to the Venedi, at the source of the Save and Drave. In 833, Ansgarius preached in Denmark, Gaudibert in Sweden, and about 861, Methodius and Cyril, in Bohemia.

About the year 500, the Scythians over-run Bulgaria, and Christianity was extirpated; but about 870 they were re-converted. Poland began to be brought over about the same time, and afterwards, about 960 or 990, the work was further extended amongst the Poles and Prussians. The work was begun in Norway in 960, and in Muscovy in 989, the Swedes propagated Christianity in Finland, in 1168, Lithuania became Christian in 1386, and Samogitia in 1439. The Spaniards forced popery upon the inhabitants of South-America, and the Portuguese in Asia. The Jesuits were sent into China in 1552. Xavier, whom they call the apostle of the Indians, laboured in the East-Indies and Japan, from 1541 to 1552, and several millions of Capauchins were sent to Africa in the seventeenth century. But blind zeal, gross superstition, and infamous cruelties, so marked the appearances of religion all this time, that the professors of Christianity needed conversion, as much as the heathen world.

A few pious people had fled from the general corruption, and lived obscurely in the vallies of Piedmont and Savoy, who were like the seed of the church. Some of them were now and then necessitated to travel into other parts, where they faithfully testified against the corruptions of the times. About 1369 Wickliffe began to preach the faith in England, and his preaching and writings were the means of the conversion of great numbers, many of whom became excellent preachers; and a work was begun which afterwards spread in England, Hungary, Bohemia, Germany, Switzerland, and many other places. John Huss and Jerom of Prague, preached boldly and successfully in Bohemia, and the adjacent parts. In the following century Luther, Calvin, Melancton, Bucer, Martyr, and many others, stood up against all the rest of the world; they preached, and prayed, and wrote; and nations agreed one after another to cast off the yoke of popery, and to embrace the doctrine of the gospel.

In England, episcopal tyranny succeeded to popish cruelty, which, in the year 1620, obliged many pious people to leave their native land and settle in America; these were followed by others in 1629, who laid the foundations of several gospel churches, which have increased amazingly since that time, and the Redeemer has fixed his throne in that country, where but a little time ago, Satan had universal dominion.

In 1632, Mr. Elliot, of New-England, a very pious and zealous minister, began to preach to the Indians, among whom he had great success; several churches of Indians were planted, and some preachers and school-masters raised up amongst them; since which time others have laboured amongst them with some good encouragement. About the year 1743, Mr. David Brainerd was sent a missionary to some more Indians, where he preached, and prayed, and after some time an extraordinary work of conversion was wrought, and wonderful success attended his ministry. And at this present time, Mr. Kirkland and Mr. Sergeant are employed in the same good work, and God has considerably blessed their labours.

In 1706, the king of Denmark sent a Mr. Ziegenbalg, and some others, to Tranquebar, on the Coromandel coast in the East-Indies, who were useful to the natives, so that many of the heathens were turned to the Lord. The Dutch East-India Company likewise having extended their commerce, built the city of Batavia, and a church was opened there; and the Lord's Supper was administered for the first time, on the 3d of January, 1621, by their minister James Hulzibos, from hence some ministers were sent to Amboyna, who were very successful. A seminary of learning was erected at Leyden, in which ministers and assistants were educated, under the renowned *Walaeus*, and some years a great number were sent to the East, at the Company's expence, so that in a little time many thousands at Formosa, Malabar, Ternate, Jaffanapatnam, in the town of Columba, at Amboyna, Java, Banda, Macassar, and Malabar, embraced the religion of our Lord Jesus Christ. The work has decayed in some places, but they now have churches in Ceylon, Sumatra, Java, Amboyna, and some other of the spice islands, and at the Cape of Good Hope, in Africa.

But none of the moderns have equalled the Moravian Brethren in this good work; they have sent missions to Greenland, Labrador, and several of the West-Indian Islands, which have been blessed for good. They have likewise sent to Abyssinia, in Africa, but what success they have had I cannot tell.

The late Mr. Wesley lately made an effort in the West-Indies, and some of their ministers are now labouring amongst the Caribbs and Negroes, and I have seen pleasing accounts of their success.

# SECT. III.

*Containing a Survey of the present State of the World.*

In this survey I shall consider the world as divided, according to its usual division, into four parts, *EUROPE, ASIA, AFRICA,* and *AMERICA,* and take notice of the extent of the several countries, their population, civilization, and religion. The article of religion I shall divide into Christian, Jewish, Mahometan, and Pagan; and shall now and then hint at the particular sect of them that prevails in the places which I shall describe. The following Tables will exhibit a more comprehensive view of what I propose, than any thing I can offer on the subject.

## *EUROPE.*

| Countries. | EXTENT Length Miles. | Breadth Miles. | Number of Inhabitants. | Religion. |
|---|---|---|---|---|
| Great-Britain | 680 | 300 | 12,000,000 | Protestants, of many denominations. |
| Ireland | 285 | 160 | 2,000,000 | Protestants and Papists. |
| France | 600 | 500 | 24,000,000 | Catholics, Deists, and Protestants. |
| Spain | 700 | 500 | 9,500,000 | Papists. |
| Portugal | 300 | 100 | 2,000,000 | Papists. |
| Sweden, *including* Sweden proper, Gothland, Shonen, Lapland, Bothnia, and Finland | 800 | 500 | 3,500,000 | The Swedes are serious Lutherans, but most of the Laplanders are Pagans, and very superstitious. |
| Isle of Gothland | 80 | 23 | 5,000 | |
| —— Oesel | 45 | 24 | 2,500 | |
| —— Oeland | 84 | 9 | 1,000 | |
| —— Dago | 26 | 23 | 1,000 | |
| —— Aland | 24 | 20 | 800 | |
| —— Hogland | 9 | 5 | 100 | |
| Denmark | 240 | 114 | 360,000 | Lutherans of the Helvetic Confession. |

| | | | | |
|---|---|---|---|---|
| Isle of Zeeland | 60 | 60 | 284,000 | Ditto. |
| —— Funen | 38 | 32 | 144,000 | Ditto. |
| —— Arroe | 8 | 2 | 200 | Ditto. |
| —— Iceland | 435 | 185 | 60,000 | Ditto. |
| —— Langeland | 27 | 12 | 3,000 | Ditto. |
| —— Laland | 38 | 30 | 148,000 | Ditto. |
| —— Falster | 27 | 12 | 3,000 | Ditto. |
| —— Mona | 14 | 5 | 600 | Ditto. |
| —— Alsen | 15 | 6 | 600 | Ditto. |
| —— Femeren | 13 | 8 | 1,000 | Ditto. |
| —— Bornholm | 20 | 12 | 2,000 | Lutherans. |
| Greenland | *Undiscovered.* | | 7,000 | Pagans, and Moravian Christians. |
| Norway | 750 | 170 | 724,000 | Lutherans. |
| 24 Faro Isles | | | 4,500 | Ditto. |
| Danish Lapland | 285 | 172 | 100,000 | Ditto, and Pagans. |
| Poland | 700 | 680 | 9,000,000 | Papists, Lutherans, Calvinists, & Jews. |
| Prussia[4] | 400 | 160 | 2,500,000 | Calvinists, Catholics, & Lutherans. |
| Sardinia | 135 | 57 | 600,000 | Papists. |
| Sicily | 180 | 92 | 1,000,000 | Ditto. |
| Italy | 660 | 120 | 20,000,000 | Ditto. |
| United Netherlands | 150 | 150 | 2,000,000 | Protestants of several denominations. |
| Austrian Netherlands | 200 | 200 | 2,500,000 | Papists and Protestants. |
| Switzerland | 200 | 100 | 2,880,000 | Papists and Protestants. |
| The Grisons. | 100 | 62 | 800,000 | Lutherans and Papists. |
| The Abbacy of St. Gall | 24 | 10 | 50,000 | Ditto. |
| Neufchatel | 32 | 20 | 100,000 | Calvinists. |
| Valais | 80 | 30 | 440,000 | Papists. |
| Piedmont | 140 | 98 | 900,000 | Ditto, and Protestants. |
| Savoy | 87 | 60 | 720,000 | Ditto. |
| Geneva, City | | | 24,000 | Calvinists. |
| Bohemia | 478 | 322 | 2,100,000 | Papists and Moravians. |

---

[4] The rest of the Prussian dominions being scattered about in several countries, are counted to those countries where they lie.

| | | | | |
|---|---|---|---|---|
| Hungary | 300 | 200 | 2,500,000 | Papists. |
| Germany | 600 | 500 | 20,000,000 | Ditto, and Protestants. |
| Russia in Europe | 1500 | 1100 | 22,000,000 | Greek Church. |
| Turkey in Europe | 1000 | 900 | 18,000,000 | Greek Christians, Jews, & Mahometans. |
| Budziac Tartary | 300 | 60 | 1,200,000 | Greek Christians, Jews, & Mahometans. |
| Lesser Tartary | 390 | 65 | 1,000,000 | Ditto. |
| Crim Tartary | 145 | 80 | 500,000 | Ditto. |
| Isle of Tenedos | 5 | 3 | 200 | Mahometans. |
| —— Negropont | 90 | 25 | 25,000 | Ditto. |
| —— Lemnos | 25 | 25 | 4,000 | Ditto. |
| —— Paros | 36 in compass. | | 4,500 | Greek Christians. |
| —— Lesbos, or Mitylene | 160 in compass. | | 30,000 | Mahometans and Greeks. |
| —— Naxia | 100 in compass. | | 8,000 | Greeks and Papists. |
| —— Scio, or Chios | 112 in compass. | | 113,000 | Greek Christians, Papists, & Mahomet. |
| —— Nio | 40 in compass. | | 1,000 | Ditto. |
| —— Scyros | 60 in compass. | | 1,000 | Ditto. |
| —— Mycone | 36 in compass. | | 3,000 | Ditto. |
| —— Samos | 30 | 15 | 12,000 | Mahometans. |
| —— Nicaria | 70 in compass. | | 3,000 | Greek Christians. |
| —— Andros | 120 in compass. | | 4,000 | Ditto. |
| —— Cyclades, *Delos the Chief* | | | 700 | Ditto. |
| —— Zia | 40 in compass. | | 8,000 | Ditto. |
| —— Cerigo or Cytheraea | 50 in compass. | | 1,000 | Ditto. |
| —— Santorin | 36 in compass. | | 10,000 | Ditto, and Papists. |
| —— Policandra | 8 in compass. | | 400 | Ditto. |
| —— Patmos | 18 in compass. | | 600 | Ditto. |
| —— Sephanto | 36 in compass. | | 5,000 | Greeks. |
| —— Claros | 40 in compass. | | 1,700 | Mahometans. |
| —— Amorgo | 36 in compass. | | 4,000 | Greek Christians. |
| —— Leros | 18 in compass. | | 800 | Christians and Mahometans. |
| —— Thermia | 40 in compass. | | 6,000 | Greek Christians. |

| | | | | |
|---|---|---|---|---|
| —— Stampalia | 50 in compass. | | 3,000 | Ditto. |
| —— Salamis | 50 in compass. | | 1,000 | Ditto. |
| —— Scarpanta | 20 in compass. | | 2,000 | Ditto. |
| —— Cephalonia | 130 in compass. | | 50,000 | Ditto. |
| —— Zant | 50 in compass. | | 30,000 | Greek Christians. |
| —— Milo | 60 in compass. | | 40,000 | Ditto. |
| —— Corfu | 120 in compass. | | 60,000 | Ditto. |
| —— Candia, or Crete | 200 | 60 | 400,000 | Ditto, and Mahometans. |
| —— Coos, or Stanchia | 70 in compass. | | 12,800 | Mahometans and Christians. |
| —— Rhodes | 60 | 25 | 120,000 | Ditto. |
| —— Cyprus | 150 | 70 | 300,000 | Mahometans. |

# ASIA.

| Countries. | EXTENT Length Miles. | Breadth Miles. | Number of Inhabitants. | Religion. |
|---|---|---|---|---|
| Turkey in Asia *contains* Anatolia, Syria, Palestine, Diabekr, Turcomania, and Georgia | 1000 | 800 | 20,000,000 | Mahometanism is most prevalent, but there are many Greek, Latin, Eutychian, and Armenian Christians. |
| Arabia | 1300 | 1200 | 16,000,000 | Mahometans. |
| Persia | 1280 | 1140 | 20,000,000 | Ditto, of the Sect of Ali. |
| Great Tartary | 4000 | 1200 | 40,000,000 | Mahometans and Pagans. |
| Siberia | 2800 | 9600 | 7,500,000 | Greek Christians and Pagans. |
| Samojedia | 2000 | 370 | 1,900,000 | Pagans. |
| Kamtschatcha | 540 | 236 | 900,000 | Ditto. |
| Nova Zembla | *Undiscovered.* | thinly inhabit. | Ditto. | |
| China | 1400 | 1260 | 60,000,000 | Ditto. |
| Japan *contains* Niphon Isl. | 900 | 360 | 10,000,000 | Ditto. |
| Isle of Ximo | 210 | 200 | 3,000,000 | Pagans. |
| —— Xicoco | 117 | 104 | 1,800,000 | Ditto. |
| —— Tsussima | 39 | 34 | 40,000 | Ditto. |
| —— Iki | 20 | 17 | 6,000 | Ditto. |
| —— Kubitessima | 30 | 26 | 8,000 | Ditto. |
| —— Matounsa | 54 | 26 | 50,000 | Ditto. |
| —— Fastistia | 36 | 34 | 30,000 | Ditto. |
| —— Firando | 30 | 28 | 10,000 | Ditto. |
| —— Amacusa | 27 | 24 | 6,000 | Ditto. |
| —— Awasi | 30 | 18 | 5,000 | Ditto. |
| India *beyond the Ganges* | 2000 | 1000 | 50,000,000 | Mahometans and Pagans. |
| Indostan | 2000 | 1500 | 110,000,000 | Ditto. |
| Tibet | 1200 | 480 | 10,000,000 | Pagans. |

| | | | | |
|---|---|---|---|---|
| Isle of Ceylon | 250 | 200 | 2,000,000 | Pagans, except the Dutch Christians. |
| —— Maldives | 1000 *in number.* | 100,000 | Mahometans . | |
| —— Sumatra | 1000 | 100 | 2,100,000 | Ditto, and Pagans. |
| —— Java | 580 | 100 | 2,700,000 | Ditto. |
| —— Timor | 2400 | 54 | 300,000 | Ditto, and a few Christians. |
| —— Borneo | 800 | 700 | 8,000,000 | Ditto. |
| —— Celebes | 510 | 240 | 2,000,000 | Ditto. |
| —— Boutam | 75 | 30 | 80,000 | Mahometans. |
| —— Carpentyn | 30 | 3 | 2,000 | Christian Protestants. |
| —— Ourature | 18 | 6 | 3,000 | Pagans. |
| —— Pullo Lout | 60 | 36 | 10,000 | Ditto. |

Besides the little Islands of Manaar, Aripen, Caradivia, Pengandiva, Analativa, Nainandiva, and Nindundiva, which are inhabited by Christian Protestants.

And Banca, Madura, Bally, Lambeck, Flores, Solor, Leolana, Panterra, Miscomby, and several others, inhabited by Pagans and Mahometans.

The Moluccas are,

| | | | | |
|---|---|---|---|---|
| —— Banda | 20 | 10 | 6,000 | Pagans and Mahometans. |
| —— Buro | 25 | 10 | 7,000 | Ditto. |

| | | | | |
|---|---|---|---|---|
| —— Amboyna | 25 | 10 | 7,500 | Christians;—the Dutch have 25 Ch. |
| —— Ceram | 210 | 45 | 250,000 | Pagans and Mahometans. |
| —— Gillola | 190 | 110 | 650,000 | Ditto. |
| And Pullo-way, Pullo-rin, Nera, Guamanapi, Guilliaien, Ternate, Metir, Machian, and Bachian, which are inhabited by Pagans and Mahometans. | | | | |
| The Phillippine Islands are supposed to be about 11,000;—some of the chief are, | | | | |
| Isle of Mindanao | 60 | 40 | 18,000 | Pagans and Mahometans. |
| —— Bahol | 24 | 12 | 6,000 | Ditto. |
| —— Layta | 48 | 27 | 10,000 | Ditto. |
| —— Parragon | 240 | 60 | 100,000 | Ditto. |
| The Calamines are Sebu | 60 | 24 | 10,000 | Papists. |
| —— Mindora | 60 | 36 | 12,000 | Pagans and Mahometans. |
| —— Philippina | 185 | 120 | 104,000 | Ditto. |
| —— Negroes Isle | 150 | 60 | 80,000 | Papists. |
| —— Manilla | | | 31,000 | Ditto, and Pagans. |
| The Ladrone Islands are inhabited by most uncivilized Pagans. | | | | |
| New Holland | 2500 | 2000 | 12,000,000 | Pagans;—1 or 2 Ministers are there. |

| Country | Length Miles | Breadth Miles | Number of Inhabitants | Religion |
|---|---|---|---|---|
| New Zealand[5] | 960 | 180 | 1,120,000 | Ditto. |
| New Guinea | 1000 | 360 | 1,900,000 | Ditto. |
| New Britain | 180 | 120 | 900,000 | Ditto. |
| New Ireland | 180 | 60 | 700,000 | Ditto. |
| Onrong Java | *A Cluster of Isles.* | | Ditto. | |
| New Caledonia | 260 | 30 | 170,000 | Ditto. |
| New Hebrides | | | | Ditto. |
| Friendly Isles | 20 *in number.* | | Ditto. | |
| Sandwich Isles | 7 *in number.* | 400,000 | Ditto. | |
| Society Isles | 6 *in number.* | 800,000 | Ditto. | |
| Kurile Isles | 45 *in number.* | 50,000 | Ditto. | |
| Pelew Isles | | | Pagans. | |
| Oonalashka Isle | 40 | 20 | 3,000 | Ditto. |
| The other South-Sea Islands. | | | Ditto. | |

## AFRICA.

| Countries. | EXTENT Length Miles. | Breadth Miles. | Number of Inhabitants. | Religion. |
|---|---|---|---|---|
| Egypt | 600 | 250 | 2,200,000 | Mahometans and Jews. |
| Nubia | 940 | 600 | 3,000,000 | Ditto. |
| Barbary | 1800 | 500 | 3,500,000 | Mahometans, Jews, and Christians. |
| Biledulgerid | 2500 | 350 | 3,500,000 | Mahometans, Christians, and Jews. |
| Zaara, or the Desart | 3400 | 660 | 800,000 | Ditto. |
| Abyssinia | 900 | 800 | 5,800,000 | Armenian Christians. |
| Abex | 540 | 130 | 1,600,000 | Christians and Pagans. |
| Negroland | 2200 | 840 | 18,000,000 | Pagans. |
| Loango | 410 | 300 | 1,500,000 | Ditto. |
| Congo | 540 | 220 | 2,000,000 | Ditto. |
| Angola | 360 | 250 | 1,400,000 | Ditto. |
| Benguela | 430 | 180 | 1,600,000 | Ditto. |
| Mataman | 450 | 240 | 1,500,000 | Ditto. |

---

[5] [Two Islands.]

| | | | | |
|---|---|---|---|---|
| Ajan | 900 | 300 | 2,500,000 | Ditto. |
| Zanguebar | 1400 | 350 | 3,000,000 | Ditto. |
| Monoemugi | 900 | 660 | 2,000,000 | Ditto. |
| Sofala | 480 | 300 | 1,000,000 | Pagans. |
| Terra de Natal | 600 | 350 | 2,000,000 | Ditto. |
| Caffraria, or the Hottentots Country | 708 | 660 | 2,000,000 | Ditto, & a few Christians at the Cape. |
| Isle of Madagascar | 1000 | 220 | 2,000,000 | Pagans and Mahometans. |
| —— St. Mary | 54 | 9 | 5,000 | French Papists. |
| —— Mascarin | 39 | 30 | 17,000 | Ditto. |
| —— St. Helena | 21 in compass. | | 1,000 | English and French Christians. |
| —— Annabon | 16 | 14 | 4,000 | Portuguese Papists. |
| —— St. Thomas | 25 | 23 | 9,000 | Pagans. |
| —— Zocotora | 80 | 54 | 10,000 | Mahometans. |
| —— Comora Isles | 5 *in number*. | | 5,000 | Ditto. |
| —— Mauritius | 150 in compass. | | 10,000 | French Papists. |
| —— Bourbon | 90 in compass. | | 15,000 | French Papists. |
| —— Madeiras | 3 *in number*. | | 10,000 | Papists. |
| —— Cape Verd Isles | 10 *in number*. | | 20,000 | Ditto. |
| —— Canaries | 12 *in number*. | | 30,000 | Ditto. |
| —— Azores | 9 *in number*. | | 100,000 | Ditto. |
| —— Maltha | 15 | 8 | 1,200 | Ditto. |

## AMERICA.

| Countries. | EXTENT Length Breadth Miles. Miles. | | Number of Inhabitants. | Religion. |
|---|---|---|---|---|
| Brazil | 2900 | 900 | 14,000,000 | Pagans and Papists. |
| Paraguay | 1140 | 460 | 10,000,000 | Pagans. |
| Chili | 1200 | 500 | 2,000,000 | Pagans and Papists. |
| Peru | 1800 | 600 | 10,000,000 | Pagans and Papists. |
| Country of the Amazons | 1200 | 900 | 8,000,000 | Pagans. |
| Terra Firma | 1400 | 700 | 10,000,000 | Pagans and Papists. |
| Guiana | 780 | 480 | 2,000,000 | Ditto. |
| Terra Magellanica | 1400 | 460 | 9,000,000 | Pagans. |
| Old Mexico | 2220 | 600 | 13,500,000 | Ditto, and Papists. |

| | | | | |
|---|---|---|---|---|
| New Mexico | 2000 | 1000 | 14,000,000 | Ditto. |
| The States of America | 1000 | 600 | 3,700,000 | Christians, of various denominations. |
| Terra de Labrador, Nova-Scotia, Louisiana, Canada, and all the country inland from Mexico to Hudson's-Bay | 1680 | 600 | 8,000,000 | Christians, of various denominations, but most of the North-American Indians are Pagans. |
| California, and from thence along the western coast to 70 degrees south latitude, and so far inland as to meet the above article | 2820 | 1380 | 9,000,000 | Pagans. |
| All to the north of 70 degrees | unknown. | | | Pagans. |
| Cape Breton | 400 | 110 | 20,000 | Christians. |
| —— Newfoundland | 350 | 200 | 1,400 | Protestants. |
| —— Cumberland's Isle | 780 | 300 | 10,000 | Pagans. |
| —— Madre de Dios | 105 | 30 | 8,000 | Ditto. |
| —— Terra del Fuego | 120 | 36 | 5,000 | Ditto. |
| All the Islands in the Vicinity of Cape Horn | | | | Pagans. |
| The Bermudas extend | 16 | 5 | 20,000 | Half English, and Half Slaves. |
| The Little Antilles | | | | |
| are Aruba | 5 | 3 | 200 | Dutch, and Pagan Negoes. |
| —— Curassoa | 30 | 10 | 11,000 | Ditto. |
| —— Bonaire | 10 | 3 | 300 | Ditto. |
| —— Margaritta | 40 | 24 | 18,000 | Spaniards, and Pagan Negroes. |
| —— St Trinidad | 90 | 60 | 100,000 | Ditto. |
| The Bahamas are | | | | |
| —— Bahama | 50 | 16 | 16,000 | Pagans. |
| —— Providence | 28 | 11 | 6,000 | Ditto. |
| Besides Eluthera, Harbour, Lucayonegua, Andross Cigateo, Guanaliana, Yumeta, Samana, Yuma, Mayaguana, Ynguana, Caieos, and Triangula—Pagans. | | | | |
| The Antilles are | | | | |
| —— Cuba | 700 | 60 | 1,000,000 | Papists. |
| —— Jamaica | 140 | 60 | 400,000 | English, and Pagan Negroes. |

| | | | Whites. | Negroes. | |
|---|---|---|---|---|---|
| —— St. Domingo | 450 | 150 | 1,000,000 | | French, Spaniards, and Negroes. |
| —— Porto Rico | 100 | 49 | 300,000 | | Spaniards and Negroes. |
| —— Vache, or Cows I. | 18 | 2 | 1,000 | | Ditto. |

The Virgin Isles are 12 *in number*, of which Danes Island is the principal—Protestants.
The Carribbees are

| | | | Whites. | Negroes. | |
|---|---|---|---|---|---|
| —— St. Cruz | 30 | 10 | 13,500 | | Danish Protestants. |
| —— Anguilla | 30 | 9 | 6,000 | | Protestants, and Negroes. |
| —— St. Martin | 21 | 12 | 7,500 | | Ditto. |
| —— St. Bartholomew | 6 | 4 | 720 | | Ditto. |
| —— Barbuda | 20 | 12 | 7,500 | | Ditto. |
| —— Saba | 5 | 4 | 1,500 | | Ditto. |
| —— Guardulope | 45 | 38 | 50,000 | | Catholics, and Pagan Negroes. |
| —— Marigalante | 15 | 12 | 5,400 | | Ditto. |
| —— Tobago | 32 | 9 | 2,400 | | Ditto. |
| —— Desiada | 12 | 6 | 1,500 | | Ditto. |
| —— Granada | 30 | 15 | 13,500 | | English, and Pagan Negroes. |
| —— St. Lucia | 23 | 12 | 5,000 | | Ditto, and Native Pagan Caribbs. |
| | | | *Whites.* | *Negroes.* | |
| —— St. Eustatia | 6 | 4 | 5,000 | 15,000 | Dutch, English, &c. |
| —— St. Christopher | 20 | 7 | 6,000 | 36,000 | English. |
| —— Nevis | 6 | 4 | 5,000 | 10,000 | Ditto. |
| —— Antigua | 20 | 20 | 7,000 | 30,000 | Ditto. |
| —— Montferrat | 6 | 6 | 5,000 | 10,000 | Ditto. |
| —— Martinico | 60 | 30 | 20,000 | 50,000 | French. |
| —— St. Vincent's | 24 | 18 | 8,000 | 5,000 | The 8,000 are Native Caribbs. |
| —— Barbadoes | 21 | 14 | 30,000 | 100,000 | English. |
| —— Dominica | 28 | 13 | | 40,000 | Ditto, 2,000 of them Native Caribbs. |
| —— St. Thomas | 15 in compass. | | | 8,000 | Danish Protestants. |

This, as nearly as I can obtain information, is the state of the world; though in many countries, as Turkey, Arabia, Great Tartary, Africa, and America, except the United States, and most of the Asiatic Islands, we have no accounts of the number of inhabitants, that can be relied on. I have therefore only calculated the extent, and counted a certain number on an average upon a square mile; in some countries more, and in others less, according as circumstances determine. A few general remarks upon it will conclude this section.

First, the inhabitants of the world according to this calculation, amount to about seven hundred and thirty-one millions; four hundred and twenty millions of whom are still in pagan darkness; an hundred and thirty millions the followers of Mahomet; an hundred millions catholics; forty-four millions protestants; thirty millions of the greek and armenian churches, and perhaps seven millions of jews. It must undoubtedly strike every considerate mind, what a vast proportion of the sons of Adam there are, who yet remain in the most deplorable state of heathen darkness, without any means of knowing the true God, except what are afforded them by the works of nature; and utterly destitute of the knowledge of the gospel of Christ, or of any means of obtaining it. In many of these countries they have no written language, consequently no Bible, and are only led by the most childish customs and traditions. Such, for instance, are all the middle and back parts of North America, the inland parts of South America, the South-Sea Islands, New Holland, New Zealand, New Guinea; and I may add Great Tartary, Siberia, Samojedia, and the other parts of Asia contiguous to the frozen sea; the greatest part of Africa, the island of Madagascar, and many places beside. In many of these parts also they are cannibals, feeding upon the flesh of their slain enemies, with the greatest brutality and eagerness. The truth of this was ascertained, beyond a doubt, by the late eminent navigator, Cooke, of the New Zealanders, and some of the inhabitants of the western coast of America. Human sacrifices are also very frequently offered, so that scarce a week elapses without instances of this kind. They are in general poor, barbarous, naked pagans, as destitute of civilization, as they are of true religion.

Secondly, barbarous as these poor heathens are, they appear to be as capable of knowledge as we are; and in many places, at least, have discovered uncommon genius and tractableness; and I greatly question whether most of the barbarities practiced by them, have not originated in some real or supposed affront, and are therefore, more properly, acts of self-defence, than proofs of inhuman and blood-thirsty dispositions.

Thirdly, in other parts, where they have a written language, as in the East-Indies, China, Japan, &c. they know nothing of the gospel. The jesuits indeed once made many converts to popery among the Chinese; but their highest aim seemed to be to obtain their good opinion; for though the converts professed themselves Christians, yet they were allowed to honour the image of Confucius their great law-giver; and at length their ambitious intrigues brought upon them the displeasure of government, which terminated in the suppression of the mission, and almost, if not entirely, of the Christian name. It is also a melancholy fact, that the vices of Europeans have been communicated wherever they themselves have been; so that the religious state of even heathens has been rendered worse by intercourse with them!

Fourthly, a very great proportion of Asia and Africa, with some part of Europe, are *Mahometans*; and those in Persia, who are of the sect of *Hali*, are the most inveterate enemies to the Turks; and they in return abhor the Persians. The Africans are some of the most ignorant of all the mahometans; especially the Arabs, who are scattered through all the northern parts of Africa, and live upon the depredations which they are continually making upon their neighbours.

Fifthly, in respect to those who bear the Christian name, a very great degree of ignorance and immorality abounds amongst them. There are Christians, so called, of the greek and armenian churches, in all the mahometan countries; but they are, if possible, more ignorant and vicious than the mahometans themselves. The Georgian Christians, who are near the Caspian Sea, maintain themselves by selling their neighbours, relations, and children, for slaves to the Turks and Persians. And it is remarked, that if any of the greeks of Anatolia turn mussulmen, the Turks never set any store by them, on account of their being so much noted for dissimulation and hypocrisy. It is well known that most of the members of the greek church are very ignorant. Papists also are in general ignorant of divine things, and very vicious. Nor do the bulk of the church of England much exceed them, either in knowledge or holiness; and many errors, and much looseness of conduct, are to be found amongst dissenters of all denominations. The lutherans in Denmark, are much on a par with the ecclesiastics in England; and the face of most Christian countries presents a dreadful scene of ignorance, hypocrisy, and profligacy. Various baneful, and pernicious errors appear to gain ground, in almost every part of Christendom; the truths of the gospel, and even the gospel itself, are attacked, and every method that the enemy can invent is employed to undermine the kingdom of our Lord Jesus Christ.

All these things are loud calls to Christians, and especially to ministers, to exert themselves to the utmost in their several spheres of action, and to try to enlarge them as much as possible.

# SECT. IV.

*The Practicability of something being done, more than what is done, for the Conversion of the Heathen.*

The impediments in the way of carrying the gospel among the heathen must arise, I think, from one or other of the following things; —either their distance from us, their barbarous and savage manner of living, the danger of being killed by them, the difficulty of procuring the necessaries of life, or the unintelligibleness of their languages.

First, as to their distance from us, whatever objections might have been made on that account before the invention of the mariner's compass, nothing can be alledged for it, with any colour of plausibility in the present age. Men can now sail with as much certainty through the Great South Sea, as they can through the Mediterranean, or any lesser Sea. Yea, and providence seems in a manner to invite us to the trial, as there are to our knowledge trading companies, whose commerce lies in many of the places where, these barbarians dwell. At one time or other ships are sent to visit places of more recent discovery, and to explore parts the most unknown; and every fresh account of their ignorance, or cruelty, should call forth our pity, and excite us to concur with providence in seeking their eternal good. Scripture likewise seems to point out this method, *Surely the Isles shall wait for me; the ships of Tarshish first, to bring my sons from far, their silver, and their gold with them, unto the name of the Lord, thy God.* Isai. lx. 9. This seems to imply that in the time of the glorious increase of the church, in the latter days, (of which the whole chapter is undoubtedly a prophecy,) commerce shall subserve the spread of the gospel. The ships of Tarshish were trading vessels, which made voyages for traffic to various parts; thus much therefore must be meant by it, that *navigation*, especially that which is *commercial*, shall be one great mean of carrying on the work of

God; and perhaps it may imply that there shall be a very considerable appropriation of wealth to that purpose.

Secondly, as to their uncivilized, and barbarous way of living, this can be no objection to any, except those whose love of ease renders them unwilling to expose themselves to inconveniencies for the good of others.

It was no objection to the apostles and their successors, who went among the barbarous *Germans* and *Gauls*, and still more barbarous *Britons*! They did not wait for the ancient inhabitants of these countries, to be civilized, before they could be christianized, but went simply with the doctrine of the cross; and Tertullian could boast that "those parts of Britain which were proof against the Roman armies, were conquered by the gospel of Christ"—It was no objection to an Elliot, or a Brainerd, in later times. They went forth, and encountered every difficulty of the kind, and found that a cordial reception of the gospel produced those happy effects which the longest intercourse with Europeans, without it could never accomplish. It *is* no objection to commercial men. It only requires that we should have as much love to the souls of our fellow-creatures, and fellow sinners, as they have for the profits arising from a few otter-skins, and all these difficulties would be easily surmounted.

After all, the uncivilized state of the heathen, instead of affording an objection *against* preaching the gospel to them, ought to furnish an argument *for* it. Can we as men, or as christians, hear that a great part of our fellow creatures, whose souls are as immortal as ours, and who are as capable as ourselves, of adorning the gospel, and contributing by their preaching, writings, or practices to the glory of our Redeemer's name, and the good of his church, are inveloped in ignorance and barbarism? Can we hear that they are without the gospel, without government, without laws, and without arts, and sciences; and not exert ourselves to introduce amongst them the sentiments of men, and of Christians? Would not the spread of the gospel be the most effectual mean of their civilization? Would not that make them useful members of society? We know that such effects did in a measure follow the afore-mentioned efforts of *Elliot*, *Brainerd*, and others amongst the American Indians; and if similar attempts were made in other parts of the world, and succeeded with a divine blessing (which we have every reason to think they would) might we not expect to see able Divines, or read well-conducted treatises in defence of the truth, even amongst those who at present seem to be scarcely human?

Thirdly, *In respect to the danger of being killed by them*, it is true that whoever does go must put his life in his hand, and not consult with flesh and blood; but do not the goodness of the cause, the duties incumbent on us as the creatures of God, and Christians, and the perishing state of our fellow men, loudly call upon us to venture all and use every warrantable exertion for their benefit? Paul and Barnabas, who *hazarded their lives for the name of our Lord Jesus Christ*, were not blamed as being rash, but commended for so doing, while John Mark who through timidity of mind deserted them in their perilous undertaking, was branded with censure. After all, as has been already observed, I greatly question whether most of the barbarities practiced by the savages upon those who have visited them, have not originated in some real or supposed affront, and were therefore, more properly, acts of self-defence, than proofs of ferocious dispositions. No wonder if the imprudence of sailors should prompt them to offend the simple savage, and the offence be resented; but *Elliot*, *Brainerd*, and the *Moravian missionaries*, have been very seldom molested. Nay, in general the heathen have shewed a willingness to hear the word; and have principally expressed their hatred of Christianity on account of the vices of nominal Christians.

Fourthly, *As to the difficulty of procuring the necessaries of life*, this would not be so great as may appear at first sight; for though we could not procure European food, yet we might procure such as the natives of those countries which we visit, subsist upon themselves. And this would only be passing through what we have virtually engaged, in by entering on the ministerial office. A Christian minister is a person who in a peculiar sense is *not his own*; he is the *servant* of God, and therefore ought to be wholly devoted to him. By entering on that sacred office he solemnly undertakes to be always engaged, as much as possible, in the Lord's work, and not to chuse his own pleasure, or employment, or pursue the ministry as a something that is to subserve his own ends, or interests, or as a kind of bye-work. He engages to go where God pleases, and to do, or endure what he sees fit to command, or call him to, in the exercise of his function. He virtually bids farewell to friends, pleasures, and comforts, and stands in readiness to endure the greatest sufferings in the work of his Lord, and Master. It is inconsistent for ministers to please themselves with thoughts of a numerous auditory, cordial friends, a civilized country, legal protection, affluence, splendor, or even a competency. The flights, and hatred of men, and even pretended friends, gloomy prisons, and tortures, the society of barbarians of uncouth speech, miserable accommodations in wretched wildernesses, hunger, and thirst, nakedness, weariness, and painfulness, hard work, and but little worldly encouragement, should rather be the objects of their expectation. Thus the apostles acted, in the primitive times, and endured hardness, as good soldiers of Jesus Christ; and though we living in a civilized country where Christianity is protected by law, are not called to suffer these things while we continue here, yet I question whether all are justified in staying here, while so many are perishing without means of grace in other lands. Sure I am that it is entirely contrary to the spirit of the gospel, for its ministers to enter upon it from interested motives, or with great worldly expectations. On the contrary the commission is a sufficient call to them to venture all, and, like the primitive Christians, go every where preaching the gospel.

It might be necessary, however, for two, at least, to go together, and in general I should think it best that they should be married men, and to prevent their time from being employed in procuring necessaries, two, or more, other persons, with their wives and families, might also accompany them, who should be wholly employed in providing for them. In most countries it would be necessary for them to cultivate a little spot of ground just for their support, which would be a resource to them, whenever their supplies failed. Not to mention the advantages they would reap from each others company, it would take off the enormous expence which has always attended undertakings of this kind, the first expence being the whole; for though a large colony needs support for a considerable time, yet so small a number would, upon receiving the first crop, maintain themselves. They would have the advantage of choosing their situation, their wants would be few; the women, and even the children, would be necessary for domestic purposes; and a few articles of stock, as a cow or two, and a bull, and a few other cattle of both sexes, a very few utensils of husbandry, and some corn to sow their land, would be sufficient. Those who attend the missionaries should understand husbandry, fishing, fowling, &c. and be provided with the necessary implements for these purposes. Indeed a variety of methods may be thought of, and when once the work is undertaken, many things will suggest themselves to us, of which we at present can form no idea.

Fifthly, As to *learning their languages*, the same means would be found necessary here as in trade between different nations. In some cases interpreters might be obtained, who might be employed for a time; and where these were not to be found, the missionaries must have patience, and mingle with the people, till they have learned so much of their language as to be able to communicate their ideas to them in it. It is well known to require no very extraordinary talents to learn, in the space of a year, or two at most, the language of any people upon earth, so much of it at least, as to be able to convey any sentiments we wish to their understandings.

The Missionaries must be men of great piety, prudence, courage, and forbearance; of undoubted orthodoxy in their sentiments, and must enter with all their hearts into the spirit of their mission; they must be willing to leave all the comforts of life behind them, and to encounter all the hardships of a torrid, or a frigid climate, an uncomfortable manner of living, and every other inconvenience that can attend this undertaking. Clothing, a few knives, powder and shot, fishing-tackle, and the articles of husbandry above-mentioned, must be provided for them; and when arrived at the place of their destination, their first business must be to gain some acquaintance with the language of the natives, (for which purpose two would be better than one,) and by all lawful means to endeavour to cultivate a friendship with them, and as soon as possible let them know the errand for which they were sent. They must endeavour to convince them that it was their good alone, which induced them to forsake their friends, and all the comforts of their native country. They must be very careful not to resent injuries which may be offered to them, nor to think highly of themselves, so as to despise the poor heathens, and by those means lay a foundation for their resentment, or rejection of the gospel. They must take every opportunity of doing them good, and labouring, and travelling, night and day, they must instruct, exhort, and rebuke, with all long suffering, and anxious desire for them, and, above all, must be instant in prayer for the effusion of the Holy Spirit upon the people of their charge. Let but missionaries of the above description engage in the work, and we shall see that it is not impracticable.

It might likewise be of importance, if God should bless their labours, for them to encourage any appearances of gifts amongst the people of their charge; if such should be raised up many advantages would be derived from their knowledge of the language, and customs of their countrymen; and their change of conduct would give great weight to their ministrations.

# SECT. V.

*An Enquiry into the Duty of Christians in general, and what Means ought to be used, in order to promote this Work.*

If the prophecies concerning the increase of Christ's kingdom be true, and if what has been advanced, concerning the commission given by him to his disciples being obligatory on us, be just, it must be inferred that all Christians ought heartily to concur with God in promoting his glorious designs, for *he that is joined to the Lord is one spirit.*

One of the first, and most important of those duties which are incumbent upon us, is *fervent and united prayer.* However the influence of the Holy Spirit may be set at nought, and run down by many, it will be found upon trial, that all means which we can use, without it, will be ineffectual. If a temple is raised for God in the heathen world, it will not be *by might, nor by power,* nor by the authority of the magistrate, or the eloquence of the orator; *but by my Spirit, saith the Lord of Hosts.* We must therefore be in real earnest in supplicating his blessing upon our labours.

It is represented in the prophets, that when there shall be *a great mourning in the land, as the mourning of Hadadrimmon in the valley of Megiddon, and every family shall mourn apart, and their wives apart,* it shall all follow upon *a spirit of grace, and supplication.* And when these things shall take place, it is promised that *there shall be a fountain opened for the house of David, and for the inhabitants of Jerusalem, for sin, and for uncleanness,*—and that *the idols shall be destroyed,* and *the false prophets ashamed* of their profession. Zech. xii 10. 14.—xiii. 1. 6. This prophesy seems to teach that when there shall be an universal conjunction in fervent prayer, and all shall esteem Zion's welfare as their own, then copious influences of the Spirit shall be shed upon the churches, which like a purifying *fountain* shall cleanse the servants of the Lord. Nor shall this cleansing influence stop here; all old idolatrous prejudices shall be rooted out, and truth prevail so gloriously that false teachers shall be so ashamed as rather to wish to be classed with obscure herdsmen, or the meanest peasants, than bear the ignominy attendant on their detection.

The most glorious works of grace that have ever took place, have been in answer to prayer; and it is in this way, we have the greatest reason to suppose, that the glorious out-pouring of the Spirit, which we expect at last, will be bestowed.

With respect to our own immediate connections, we have within these few years been favoured with some tokens for good, granted in answer to prayer, which should encourage us to persist, and increase in that important duty. I trust our *monthly prayer-meetings* for the success of the gospel have not been in vain. It is true a want of importunity too generally attends our prayers; yet unimportunate, and feeble as they have been, it is to be believed that God has heard, and in a measure answered them. The churches that have engaged in the practice have in general since that time been evidently on the increase; some controversies which have long perplexed and divided the church, are more clearly stated than ever; there are calls to preach the gospel in many places where it has not been usually published; yea, a glorious door is opened, and is likely to be opened wider and wider, by the spread of civil and religious liberty, accompanied also by a diminution of the spirit of popery; a noble effort has been made to abolish the inhuman Slave-Trade, and though at present it has not been so successful as might be wished, yet it is to be hoped it will be persevered in, till it is accomplished. In the mean time it is a satisfaction to consider that the late defeat of the abolition of the Slave-Trade has proved the occasion of a praise worthy effort to introduce a free settlement, at *Sierra Leona*, on the coast of Africa; an effort which, if succeeded with a divine blessing, not only promises to open a way for honourable commerce with that extensive country, and for the civilization of its inhabitants, but may prove the happy mean of introducing amongst them the gospel of our Lord Jesus Christ.

These are events that ought not to be over-looked; they are not to be reckoned small things; and yet perhaps they *are* small compared with what might have been expected, if all had cordially entered into the spirit of the proposal, so as to have made the cause of Christ their own, or in other words to have been so solicitous about it, as if their own advantage depended upon its success. If an holy solicitude had prevailed in all the assemblies of Christians in behalf of their Redeemer's kingdom, we might probably have seen before now, not only an *open door* for the gospel, but *many running to and fro, and knowledge increased*; or a diligent use of those means which providence has put in our power, accompanied with a greater blessing than ordinary from heaven.

Many can do nothing but pray, and prayer is perhaps the only thing in which Christians of all denominations can cordially, and unreservedly unite; but in this we may all be one, and in this the strictest unanimity ought to prevail. Were the whole body thus animated by one soul, with what pleasure would Christians attend on all the duties of religion, and with what delight would their ministers attend on all the business of their calling.

We must not be contented however with praying, without *exerting ourselves in the use of means* for the obtaining of those things we pray for. Were *the children of light*, but *as wise in their generation as the children of this world*, they would stretch every nerve to gain so glorious a prize, nor ever imagine that it was to be obtained in any other way.

When a trading company have obtained their charter they usually go to its utmost limits; and their stocks, their ships, their officers, and men are so chosen, and regulated, as to be likely to answer their purpose; but they do not stop here, for encouraged by the prospect of success, they use every effort, cast their bread upon the waters, cultivate friendship with every one from whose information they expect the least advantage. They cross the widest and most tempestuous seas, and encounter the most unfavourable climates; they introduce themselves into the most barbarous nations, and sometimes undergo the most affecting hardships;

their minds continue in a state of anxiety, and suspence, and a longer delay than usual in the arrival of their vessels agitates them with a thousand changeful thoughts, and foreboding apprehensions, which continue till the rich returns are safe arrived in port. But why these fears? Whence all these disquietudes, and this labour? Is it not because their souls enter into the spirit of the project, and their happiness in a manner depends on its success?—Christians are a body whose truest interest lies in the exaltation of the Messiah's kingdom. Their charter is very extensive, their encouragements exceeding great, and the returns promised infinitely superior to all the gains of the most lucrative fellowship. Let then every one in his station consider himself as bound to act with all his might, and in every possible way for God.

Suppose a company of serious Christians, ministers and private persons, were to form themselves into a society, and make a number of rules respecting the regulation of the plan, and the persons who are to be employed as missionaries, the means of defraying the expence, &c. &c. This society must consist of persons whose hearts are in the work, men of serious religion, and possessing a spirit of perseverance; there must be a determination not to admit any person who is not of this description, or to retain him longer than he answers to it.

From such a society a *committee* might be appointed, whose business it should be to procure all the information they could upon the subject, to receive contributions, to enquire into the characters, tempers, abilities and religious views of the missionaries, and also to provide them with necessaries for their undertakings.

They must also pay a great attention to the views of those who undertake this work; for want of this the missions to the Spice Islands, sent by the Dutch East-India Company, were soon corrupted, many going more for the sake of settling in a place where temporal gain invited them, than of preaching to the poor Indians. This soon introduced a number of indolent, or profligate persons, whose lives were a scandal to the doctrines which they preached: and by means of whom the gospel was ejected from Ternate, in 1694, and Christianity fell into great disrepute in other places.

If there is any reason for me to hope that I shall have any influence upon any of my brethren, and fellow Christians, probably it may be more especially amongst them of my own denomination. I would therefore propose that such a society and committee should be formed amongst the *particular baptist denomination.*

I do not mean by this, in any wife to confine it to one denomination of Christians. I wish with all my heart, that every one who loves our Lord Jesus Christ in sincerity, would in some way or other engage in it. But in the present divided state of Christendom, it would be more likely for good to be done by each denomination engaging separately in the work, than if they were to embark in it conjointly. There is room enough for us all, without interfering with each other; and if no unfriendly interference took place, each denomination would bear good will to the other, and wish, and pray for its success, considering it as upon the whole friendly to the great cause of true religion; but if all were intermingled, it is likely their private discords might throw a damp upon their spirits, and much retard their public usefulness.

In respect to *contributions* for defraying the expences, money will doubtless be wanting; and suppose the rich were to embark a portion of that wealth over which God has made them stewards, in this important undertaking, perhaps there are few ways that would turn to a better account at last. Nor ought it to be confined to the *rich*; if persons in more moderate circumstances were to devote a portion, suppose a *tenth*, of their annual increase to the Lord, it would not only correspond with the practice of the Israelites, who lived under the Mosaic Oeconomy, but of the patriarchs Abraham, Isaac, and Jacob, before that dispensation commenced. Many of our most eminent fore-fathers amongst the *Puritans*, followed that practice; and if that were but attended to now, there would not only be enough to support the ministry of the gospel at home, and to encourage *village preaching* in our respective neighbourhoods, but to defray the expences of carrying the gospel into the heathen world.

If congregations were to open subscriptions of *one penny*, or more per week, according to their circumstances, and deposit it as a fund for the propogation of the gospel, much might be raised in this way. By such simple means they might soon have it in their power to introduce the preaching of the gospel into most of the villages in England; where, though men are placed whose business it should be to give light to those who sit in darkness, it is well known that they have it not. Where there was no person to open his house for the reception of the gospel, some other building might be procured for a small sum, and even then something considerable might be spared for the baptist, or other committees, for propogating the gospel amongst the heathen.

Many persons have of late left off the use of *West-India sugar* on account of the iniquitous manner in which it is obtained. Those families who have done so, and have not substituted any thing else in its place, have not only cleansed their hands of blood, but have made a saving to their families, some of six pence, and some of a shilling a week. If this, or a part of this were appropriated to the uses before-mentioned, it would abundantly suffice. We have only to keep the end in view, and have our hearts thoroughly engaged in the pursuit of it, and means will not be very difficult.

We are exhorted *to lay up treasure in heaven, where neither moth nor rust doth corrupt, nor thieves break through and steal.* It is also declared that *whatsoever a man soweth, that shall he also reap.* These Scriptures teach us that the enjoyments of the life to come, bear a near relation to that which now is; a relation similar to that of the harvest, and the seed. It is true all the reward is of mere grace, but it is nevertheless encouraging; what a *treasure*, what an *harvest* must await such characters as Paul, and Elliot, and Brainerd, and others, who have given themselves wholly to the work of the Lord. What a heaven will it be to see the many myriads of poor heathens, of Britons amongst the rest, who by their labours have been brought to the knowledge of God. Surely a *crown of rejoicing* like this is worth aspiring to. Surely it is worth while to lay ourselves out with all our might, in promoting the cause, and kingdom of Christ.

## FINIS.

www.ingramcontent.com/pod-product-compliance
Lightning Source LLC
Chambersburg PA
CBHW071751090426
42738CB00011B/2642